WHAT IS THE SOLAR SYSTEM?
ASTRONOMY BOOK FOR KIDS
Children's Astronomy Books

BABY PROFESSOR
EDUCATION KIDS

Speedy Publishing LLC

40 E. Main St. #1156

Newark, DE 19711

www.speedypublishing.com

Copyright 2017

In this book, we're going to cover interesting facts about our Solar System. So, let's get right to it!

For thousands of years, people believed that the Earth was the center of the universe. In 1543 AD, the Polish astronomer Copernicus put forth the theory that the Earth wasn't the center of the universe at all. In fact, he felt that this

"geocentric" version of the universe was all wrong. He proposed that the Sun was the center and that the planets including Earth revolved around it. This model was called the "heliocentric" model.

Earth

Eventually, astronomers discovered that not only was the Earth not the center of the planetary system, our entire Solar System and galaxy is not located at the center of the universe at all! The universe may not even have a center in the way we think of it since all the objects in it are expanding away from each other.

Our Solar System is part of a much larger group of star systems called a galaxy. The galaxy we live in is called the Milky Way. The number of stars and galaxies in the universe is such a large number that it's difficult to imagine.

Milky Way Galaxy

There are estimated to be about 200 billion stars in our galaxy alone. As for the number of galaxies, there are over 100 billion galaxies in the known universe. As telescopes improve, more and more are being found.

WHAT IS THE SOLAR SYSTEM?

Our Solar System is composed of the Sun and the other celestial bodies that revolve around it. The Sun is at the center as Copernicus had proposed and the planets, asteroids, comets, and other objects revolve around the Sun in different types of orbits.

HOW WAS OUR SOLAR SYSTEM FORMED?

Most astronomers believe that our solar system was formed from a large, molecular cloud about 4.5 billion years ago. This cloud, which was light years across, went through a gravitational collapse.

The Sun was only one of several stars that formed from this massive cloud. Eventually, Earth formed after billions of years and was pulled by the gravitational force of the Sun into its present orbit.

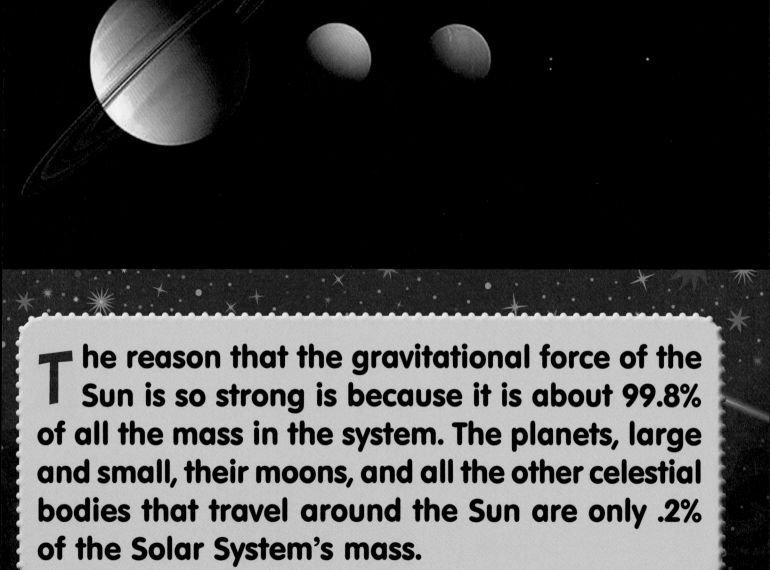

The reason that the gravitational force of the Sun is so strong is because it is about 99.8% of all the mass in the system. The planets, large and small, their moons, and all the other celestial bodies that travel around the Sun are only .2% of the Solar System's mass.

THE PLANETS

There are eight planets of varying sizes that travel around our Sun. Pluto was considered to be a planet until 2006 when it was re-categorized as a dwarf planet. Each planet is on a different cycle and orbit as it travels around the Sun.

Pluto

The paths are not perfect circles, which means that the planets are traveling in ellipses around the Sun in a counterclockwise motion. It also means there are times in the year when they are closer to the Sun and times when they are farther away. For example, the Earth is 94.5 million miles when it's at its furthest distance from the Sun and 91.4 million miles when it's the closest.

Here is a list of the eight planets in order from closest to the Sun to furthest away. The first four planets are the terrestrial planets. They have some similar characteristics because their surfaces are rocky, although their surface temperatures are not the same.

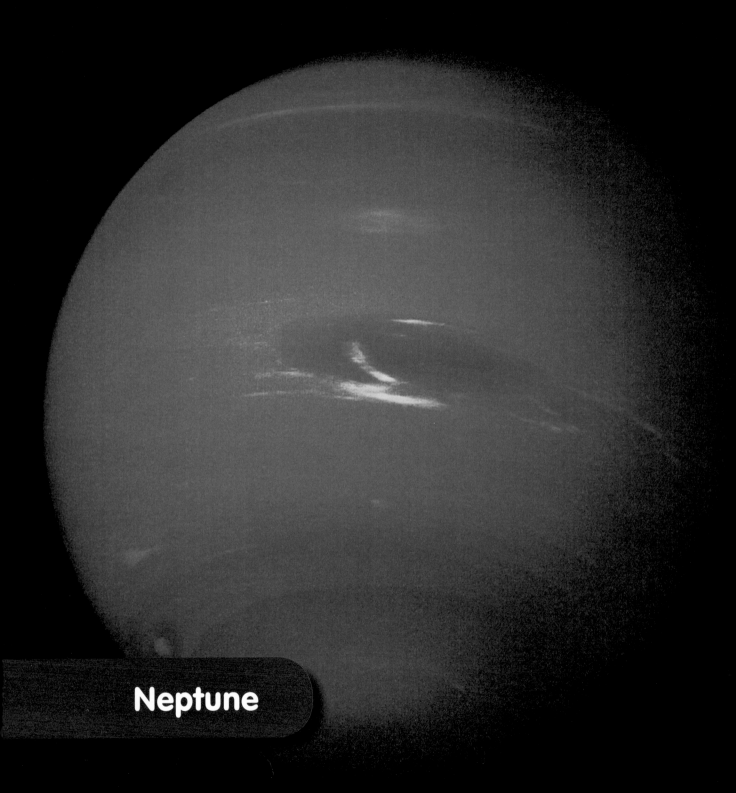
Neptune

The four planets that are located the furthest distance from the Sun are called the gas planets. Instead of being composed mostly of rock, these planets are made mostly of gases, primarily hydrogen. Both Uranus and Neptune are sometimes called "ice giants" since their composition is largely the ice form of water, ammonia, and methane.

MERCURY

The smallest planet in our Solar System, Mercury doesn't have any moons. It has a diameter of about 3,000 miles. It has a very rocky surface, next to no atmosphere, and an iron core. The surface temperature varies dramatically from minus 300 degrees Fahrenheit to 800 degrees Fahrenheit depending on which side is facing the Sun.

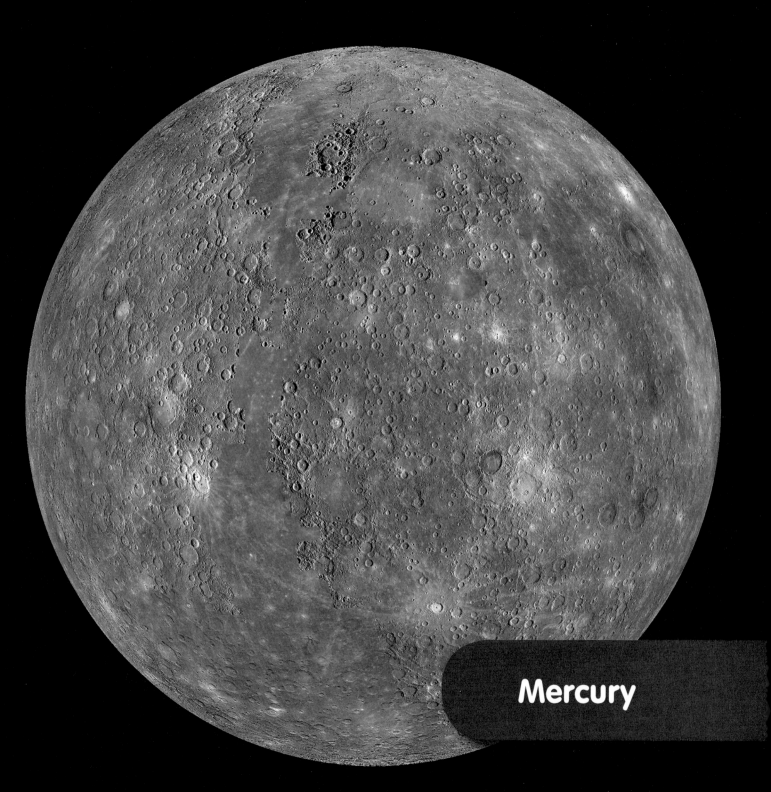

Mercury

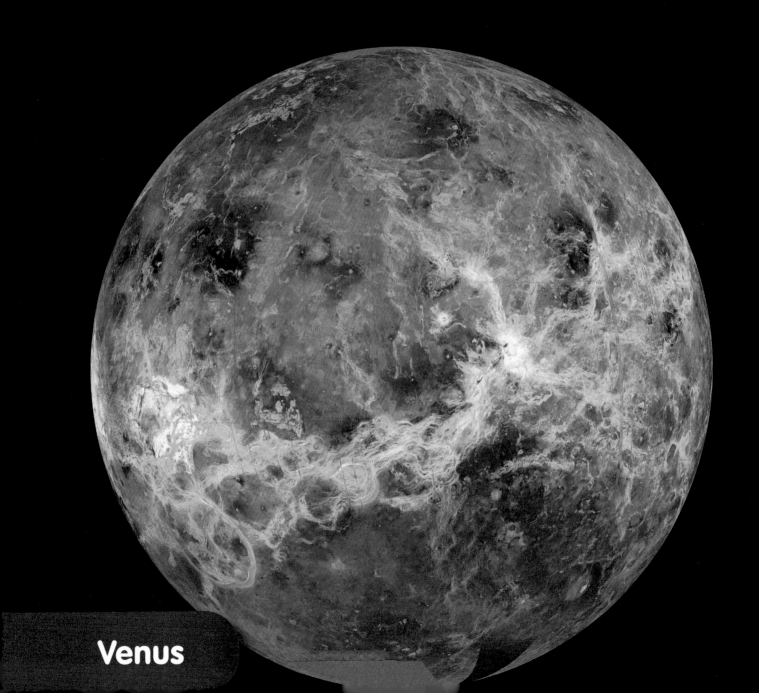
Venus

VENUS

Even though it is not as close to the Sun as Mercury, Venus is a much hotter planet. It's surrounded by carbon dioxide clouds that trap heat and don't allow it to escape. Temperatures get up to 850 degrees Fahrenheit.

Venus has no moons but other than that its geography of mountains, volcanoes, and valleys is similar to Earth. There are over 100 enormous volcanoes that throw lava out on the surface. As far as astronomers know, it has no liquid water. This planet rotates backwards from the way the other planets rotate.

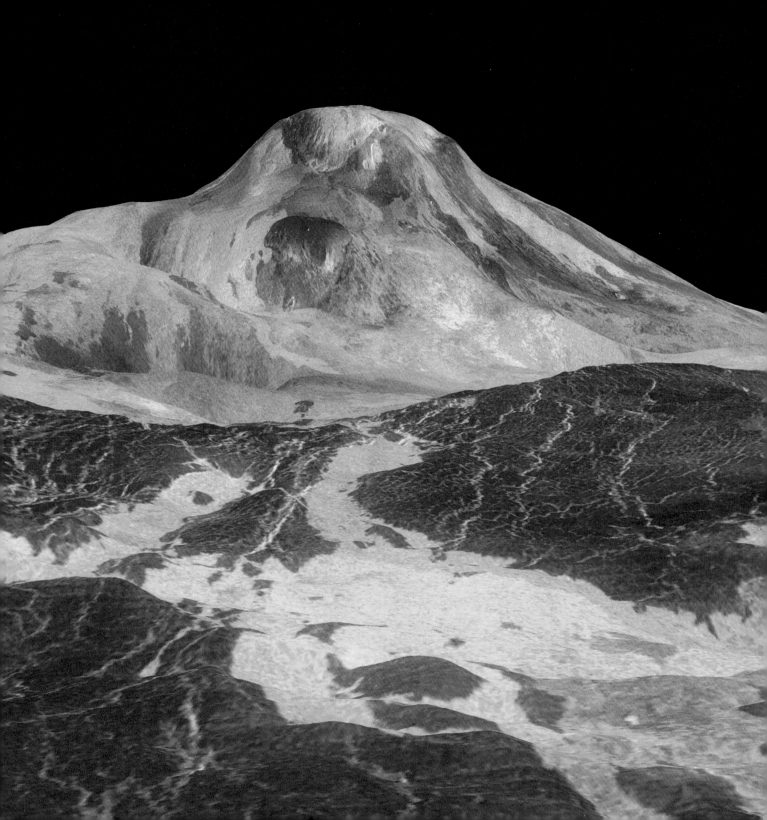

Earth

EARTH

Earth is our home and many of its features are unique among the other planets. It's the only planet that supports life. There are millions of different life forms on the seven continents and five oceans of Earth.

About 70% of the surface of our planet is made up of saltwater oceans that are teeming with life. The atmosphere is made up of the gases oxygen and nitrogen as compared to the largely CO_2 atmosphere of Venus and also Mars.

Mars

MARS

The 4th planet in terms of distance from the Sun, Mars is called the red planet due to the rusty-colored dust on its surface. Mars has huge dust storms as well as some amazing geological structures. Olympus Mons is a mountain peak that is three times the height of Mount Everest on Earth. One of its canyons, called Valles Marineris, is the largest canyon in all of our Solar System. Mars has two moons.

JUPITER

The fifth planet from the Sun, Jupiter is also the largest of the eight planets. You couldn't stand on the surface of Jupiter because its surface is made of hydrogen. Jupiter's mass is over 300 times that of Earth. Its Great Red Spot is a storm that is larger than the Earth. Jupiter has 63 moons.

Jupiter

Saturn

SATURN

The sixth planet from the Sun, the beautiful planet Saturn is known for its rings made of ice mixed with rocks and dust. Its density is less than any other planet. If you had an ocean of water that was large enough, Saturn would float on it because its density is less than water's. It has very fast winds, over 1800 kilometers per hour.

URANUS

The seventh planet from the Sun, Uranus is over fourteen times as large as Earth. It has 21 moons and has an unusual rotation compared to the other planets. Instead of spinning like a top, it rotates on its side.

Earth and Uranus

Neptune

NEPTUNE

The eighth planet from the Sun, Neptune is a large blue planet that is aptly named for the Roman god who was master of the sea. It is seventeen times as massive as the Earth and has storms that are as big as our planet.

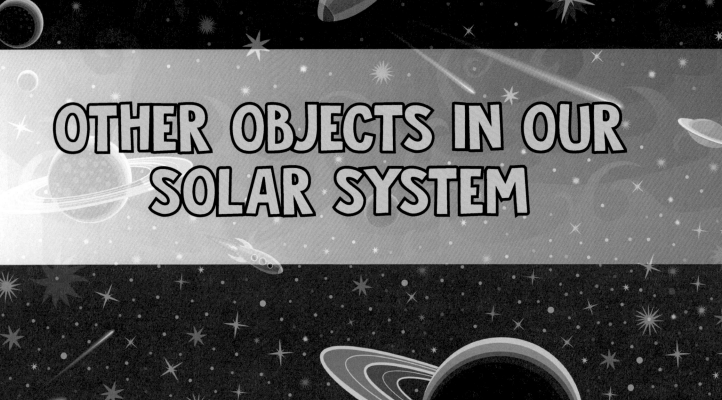

OTHER OBJECTS IN OUR SOLAR SYSTEM

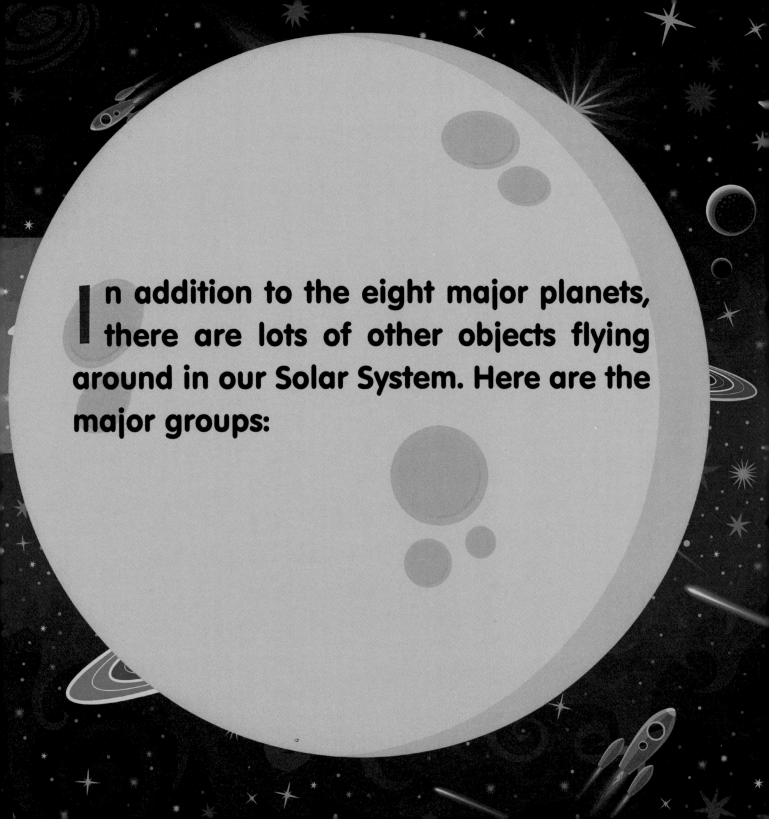

In addition to the eight major planets, there are lots of other objects flying around in our Solar System. Here are the major groups:

DWARF PLANETS

Dwarf planets are smaller than the other planets. In fact, they are so much smaller that they share their orbits with other celestial objects. Pluto is one of the dwarf planets. It has five known moons. One of the dwarf planets, called Makemake takes 310 years to make on revolution around the Sun.

Pluto

Hubble Telescope

In 2015, the Hubble telescope found that Makemake has its own tiny moon. Other dwarf planets are the moonless Ceres, located in the Asteroid Belt, Eris, which has one moon called Dysnomia, and the oddly-shaped Haumea, which has two known moons.

COMETS

Astronomers know that comets come from as far away as the Kuiper belt and possibly from the Oort Cloud as well. They are made from rocks, dust, and particles of ice. They orbit the sun in long elliptical orbits and sometimes have visible "tails."

These tails are made of gas that comes from solar radiation as well as solar wind. As of 2010, astronomers have identified at least 4,000 known comets, but there could be billions more located in the Oort Cloud.

ASTEROID BELT

The Asteroid Belt is the section of the Solar System between Mars and Jupiter. In this belt, thousands of rocks travel around the Sun. They vary greatly in size from tiny pieces to the size of Ceres, the dwarf planet.

KUIPER BELT

The Kuiper Belt is a huge amount of left-over frozen bodies from the time when our Solar System was forming. These bodies are made up of the same type of ices as the "ice planets." Thousands of these tiny objects as well as several dwarf planets are located in this belt.

OORT CLOUD

Much farther away from the Sun than the Kuiper Belt by over a thousand times, this cloud is located at the outermost edge of the Solar System. At this time, the Oort Cloud is only a theory. We don't have direct data about it because no space probe has ever been able to travel that far to send data back about it. Astronomers believe it is composed of thousands of objects made of ice.

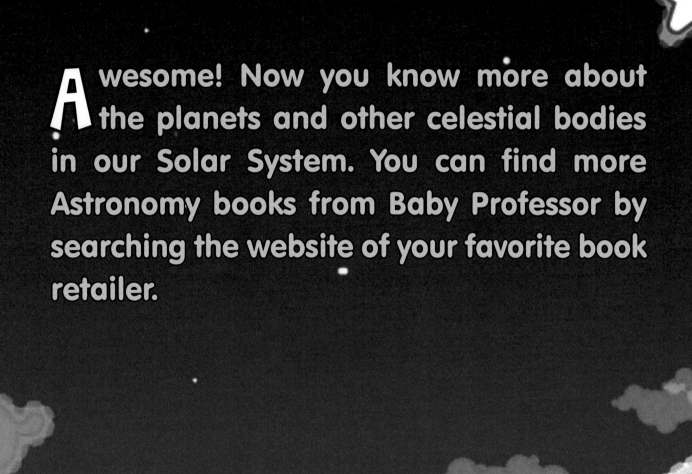

Awesome! Now you know more about the planets and other celestial bodies in our Solar System. You can find more Astronomy books from Baby Professor by searching the website of your favorite book retailer.

Made in the USA
San Bernardino, CA
09 February 2019